HOW FAST IS IT?

A Zippy Book All About Speed

by **Ben Hillman**

SCHOLASTIC

www.scholastic.com

Library of Congress Cataloging-in-Publication Data
Hillman, Ben, 1957–
   How fast is it? / by Ben Hillman.
     p. cm.
   1. Speed—Juvenile literature. I. Title.
QC137.52.H55 2008
531'.11—dc22
        2007039983

ISBN-13: 978-0-439-91867-1
ISBN-10: 0-439-91867-7

10 9 8 7 6 5 4 3 2 1   08 09 10 11 12

Printed in Singapore 46
First printing, November 2008

CONTENTS

37 miles per hour
(60 km/h)

Ostrich

See big bird run.

They say that the ostrich brain is as small as its eyeball. But this tiny brain is controlling the largest and heaviest bird in the world — which also happens to be the fastest two-legged sprinter on the planet.

If they let an ostrich run in a 10-mile (16 km) bicycle race, there would be no contest. In a match between Two Wheels and Two Legs, the legs win, hands down.

Top-notch bicyclists huff and puff to keep up a blistering pace of 25 miles per hour (40 km/h). The ostrich merely looks behind at this sorry bunch and scoffs. This bird can run up to 37 miles per hour (60 km/h) for thirty minutes nonstop — easily leaving the pathetic pedalers in the dust.

The ostrich can't fly. Running is all it does. And it has been running on this planet for at least 75 million years — back in the time of the dinosaurs — so it's pretty good at it.

For such a silly-looking bird, the ostrich running at full speed is poetry in motion. It stretches its powerful legs into long, majestic strides that leave any predator or bicyclist far behind (OK, maybe not the bike on page 23, but that's a special case). A single ostrich stride can measure up to 16 feet (5 m) long— longer than two and a half bicycles!

These powerful legs also mean that an ostrich can kick. When a lion threatens an ostrich, especially a mother ostrich guarding her eggs, that lion can end up dead.

That's an ostrich: tall, fast, deadly — and so good-looking!

361 miles per hour
(581 km/h)

Train

"Hey, Pancho."

"What, Lefty?"

"What do you say we get the gang together and rob the Kyoto Kannonball?"

Bad idea.

What foiled Pancho and Lefty's robbery attempt? These losers tried to rob a Japanese high-speed, high-tech wonder train called a *maglev* — with the record-shattering speed of 361 miles per hour (581 km/h)!

Maglev is short for *magnetic levitation*— a fancy way of saying that incredibly powerful magnets lift the train off the rails, right into the air, and shoot it down the tracks at breathtaking speed.

There are several types of maglev trains. Some have to start on regular old train wheels until they get up to speed, and some lift the train off the tracks right at start-up. When the magnets do their stuff, the magnetic force pushes the entire train up off the rails so that hundreds of tons (200,000+ kg) of steel hover up to 5 inches (13 cm) in the air! Then, using pulsed electricity, the electromagnets drive the train forward. With no friction from the rails, the train rockets to speeds unheard of for wheeled transport.

Regular trains actually *need* friction to move. It's the friction between the wheels and the track that allows the train to drag itself forward. With a maglev train, all that friction is gone — which is the key to this kind of train's blistering speed. The only thing slowing down this train is air resistance.

So forget about your Great Train Robbery. At these speeds, crime just doesn't pay.

Computer

In 2007, the supercomputer speed contest was won by IBM's BlueGene/L — an impressive machine half the size of a basketball court. But that's not the fastest computer there is. Far from it.

The fastest computer in the world is that small, squishy blob of glop inside your head.

Every year, electronic computers get faster and faster. One way to measure computer speed is in *flops*. That stands for *floating-point operations per second* (a type of calculation). The current champion machine has 65,536 chips, each chip connected to 6 other chips, resulting in a whopping 360 trillion flops (*teraflops*). Sound like a lot?

That's nothing. Your brain has 100 billion neurons, each connected to more than 10,000 other neurons, all sending messages 100 times per second. Some scientists estimate that the human brain can operate at a speed of 10 *quadrillion* flops (*petaflops*)!

No electronic computer can touch that — yet. There are new ideas in the works that could someday make computers as fast as our brains. But does speed alone mean these machines will be able to think, understand, and create like we do? No one knows.

What we do know is that the human brain enables us to perform amazing feats simultaneously — complex multitasking that today's fastest computers simply can't do: like walking down the street while listening to music while chewing gum while looking at a movie poster while talking on your cell phone, saying, "All this, like, stuff about, like, computers is, like, *sooo* bo-ring!"

10,000,000,000,000,000 flops

0.07 miles per hour
(0.11 km/h)

Sloth

The windup! The pitch! The crack of the bat! A hit! The batter sprints toward first base! Time for a nap.

If your team is winning a lot this season, it might be because one of your opposing teammates is a sloth — the slowest mammal on Earth.

If a sloth is ever lucky enough to hit a fair ball, it might move slothily toward first base at a ground speed of maybe 6 feet per minute (1.8 m/min.). This gives you and your teammates plenty of time to relax — have a drink of lemonade, catch up on some reading, or just take a catnap.

Fifteen minutes later, don't forget to jump into action! Walk over and tag the sloth out just before it reaches first base.

But we don't mean to belittle the sloth too much. Moving across the ground is not what the sloth does normally. The sloth is a tree-dweller. When it's not sleeping (up to 20 hours per day) or hanging upside down doing absolutely nothing, it slides along its branch to get to the next batch of fresh leaves to eat. Moving through the branches at a normal pace, the sloth speeds along at a breakneck 15 feet per minute (5 m/min.)!

Finally, having reached its next meal, the sloth catches its breath and resumes its leisurely lifestyle.

But sloths aren't *entirely* about laziness. When danger threatens, the sloth can shed its slothful ways and rocket through the trees at 100 feet per minute (30 m/min.).

How can it possibly recover from all that excitement? *Zzzzzzzzzzzz.*

764 miles per hour
(1,230 km/h)

Car

How fast is a fast, *fast* car?

How about faster than a screaming 747! How about fast enough to make a sonic boom with a shock wave that pulverizes the very ground it passes over!

Looking something like an airplane without wings, the Thrust SSC (that's a Thrust-powered Supersonic Car) is the first car ever to break the sound barrier.

In order to get moving that fast, the Thrust is designed from the ground up for hyperspeed. Cruising on aluminum wheels designed to withstand 35,000 g (1 g equals the force of gravity), the Thrust SSC is one amazing single-passenger vehicle! The 10.5-ton (9.5 t) car is designed around a pair of gas-gobbling Rolls-Royce Phantom jet fighter engines that produce a staggering 110,000 horsepower.

What can you do with that much raw power? Well, in the hands of British Royal Air Force pilot Andy Green, you can be the first driver to break Mach 1, reaching a ground-smashing 764 miles per hour (1,230 km/h)!

That first automotive sonic boom in history was heard on October 13, 1997, echoing across the 13-mile (21 km) course on the prehistoric dry lake bed at Black Rock Desert in Nevada — one of the flattest places on Earth.

Driving the Thrust SSC is not for the faint of heart. At top speed, letting the front of the car rise even 5 inches (13 cm) could cause the car to flip over backward. Let the front dip, and you're burrowing into the ground!

Supersonic racers, Drive with Caution!

MAY

AUGUST

Bamboo

Everyone loves a pretty window box. Plant your flowers in the spring, and by summer you'll have beautiful blossoms decorating your windowsill. Most plants grow a little bit each month, which is the reasonable thing to do.

Then there's bamboo.

If you plant a cute little bamboo shoot in your window box, you might be in for a surprise: pretty green leaves for a few days, then *phoom*! Nothing but stalk. The stalk shoots up and up, finally topping out in a burst of branches and leaves. When you plant bamboo, you've planted the fastest-growing plant in the world.

Bamboo is actually a grass. So maybe you don't want to plant it in a window box. Maybe you want to plant your lawn with it instead. Or maybe not.

In the summer you mow the grass and, if you don't like mowing, you might think it's annoying that the grass grows so fast. Maybe your grass grows about 4 inches (10 cm) per week. Well, consider yourself lucky, because if your lawn was covered in bamboo instead of regular grass, you might have to mow it *once an hour*!

Bamboo is the lightning of grass. It grows so fast that you can actually *hear* it growing! Some species of bamboo can easily grow more than 12 inches (30 cm) *per day* — rocketing up to the sky from a teeny sprout to full-grown towering maturity — as much as 80 feet (24 m) high or more — in less than three months!

Even teenagers don't grow that fast.

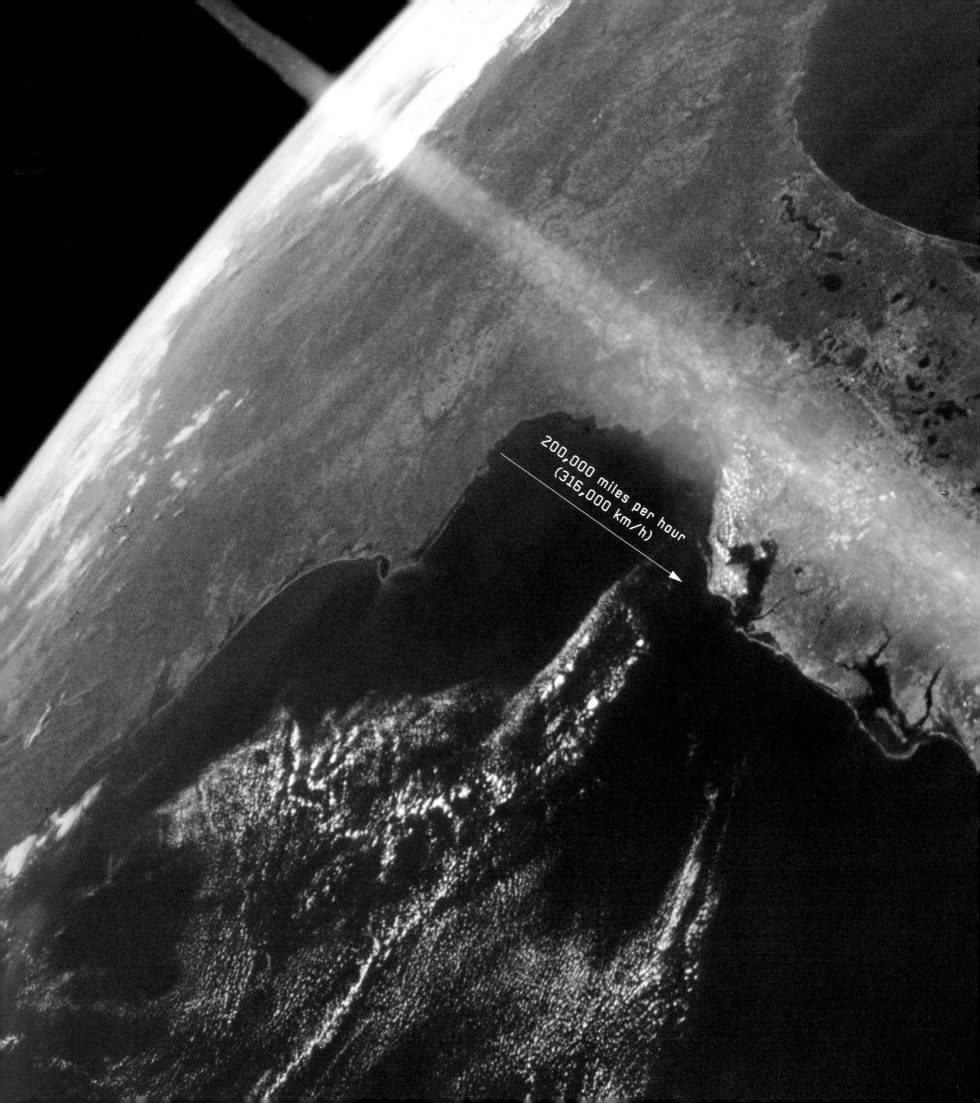

200,000 miles per hour
(316,000 km/h)

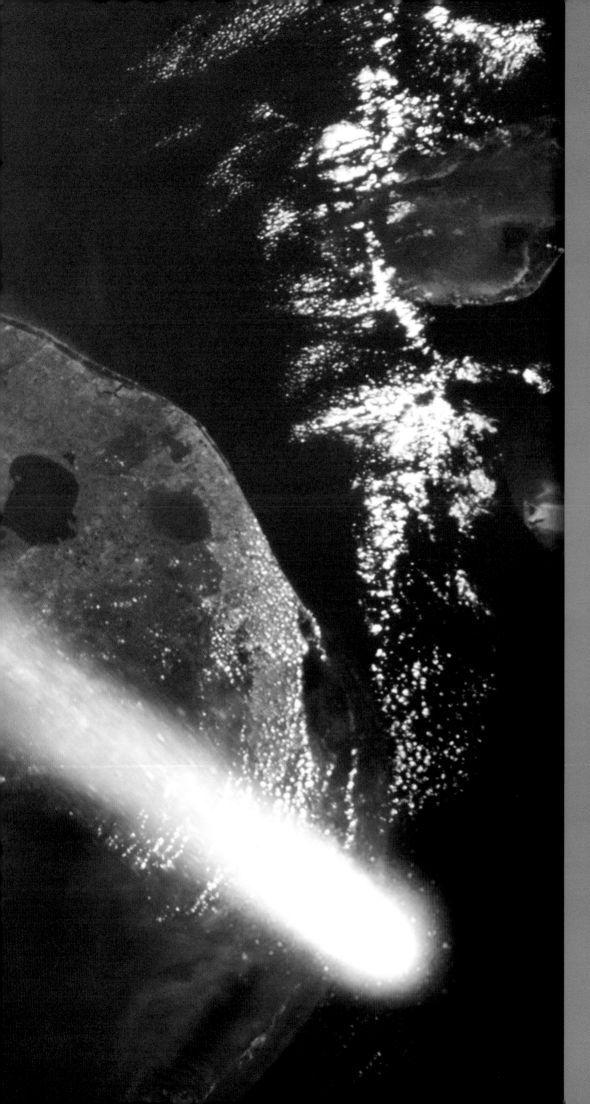

Comet

On a really cold winter's day — around 400 degrees below zero Fahrenheit (–240°C) — take some ice, mix it with some gravel, and pack it into a dirty snowball around 1.5 miles (2.5 km) wide. Then go out half a trillion miles (0.8 trillion km) into space and throw it as hard as you can toward the sun. You've made your own Comet Hyakutake!

If you threw your comet 9,000 years ago, it would arrive at the sun right on schedule in 1996 — the last time C/1996 B2 (Hyakutake) came to us for a visit.

And that visit was something to see. As the sun's gravity pulled on the comet, Hyakutake came toward us faster and faster. By the time it reached the sun, it became one of the fastest comets on record — shooting through space at just under 200,000 miles per hour (316,000 km/h). At that speed, it could travel the length of Florida in 8 seconds!

When Hyakutake came very close to the sun, our star's immense gravity whipped the comet around and flung it back into space like a slingshot. Now, as the comet leaves the sun behind, it will slow down until the sun's gravity pulls it back again for another race to the center of the solar system.

Unfortunately, we won't be seeing Hyakutake come again so soon. Its last round trip took 17,000 years or so. However, on this trip in 1996, Hyakutake came close to the giant planets Jupiter and Saturn, and its orbit was stretched out even farther.

So the next time you'll see Hyakutake streaking across the sky won't be for at least 70,000 years. Don't miss it!

17

68 miles per hour
(109 km/h)

Sailfish

Most highways have lanes for fast cars. But if they put in a lane for fast fish they'd have to make one just for the Indo-Pacific sailfish, the fastest fish in the world!

This denizen of the deep can rocket along underwater at an astounding 68 miles per hour (109 km/h)! That's three times faster than a mako shark or a dolphin! Even the speediest submarines can't go nearly as fast.

Think of how much energy it takes to make a car run at that speed on the highway. Now think of going that same speed on muscle power alone through dense water!

A cubic foot (0.03 m³) of air at sea level weighs less than 1.3 ounces (37 g). A cubic foot of water weighs more than 60 pounds (27 kg). Water is really dense stuff! More than 700 times denser than air. Yet the sailfish blasts right on through!

From one end to the other, the sailfish is designed for speed, speed, and more speed! Up in front is the long, narrow spear of bone that cuts the water while at the other end is the sailfish's unusual tail. This unique tail has a wide fork and is kept stiff by a series of interlocking vertebrae. This allows the sailfish to vibrate its tail very rapidly and shoot through the water at ultrahigh speed.

Does the sail help? Actually, sailfish keep their sails folded down most of the time, raising them when excited or alarmed. The big sail makes the fish seem larger, so it helps intimidate would-be predators.

But to catch a sailfish, that predator has to be incredibly fast. Or have a strong fishing line.

70 miles per hour
(113 km/h)

Cheetah

Some people say that cheetahs never win. We beg to differ.

If you're driving down the highway at a pokey 55 miles per hour (89 km/h), this cat will *pass* you. The cheetah is the fastest land animal alive — clocked at speeds of more than 70 miles per hour (113 km/hr).

Not only that, the cheetah can go from standing still to 45 miles per hour (72 km/h) in *two seconds* — faster than most sports cars.

How does a cat *move* that fast? The cheetah has been around for 4 million years and is the oldest member of the cat family. In that time, it had to compete with all kinds of other predators for food. The way it succeeded was with speed.

Everything in a cheetah's body is developed for speed. The cheetah's spine is flexible, storing energy like a spring and powering the cheetah's enormous strides. Running at top speed, each stride can reach upward of 25 feet (8 m) — about the length of two average cars put end to end.

The cheetah also has extra-light bones to keep it nimble; oversize lungs, liver, and heart to enable sudden bursts of energy; large nasal passages for quickly inhaling large amounts of oxygen; semiretractable claws for gripping the ground; and a long tail used for stabilization during tight turning maneuvers.

But speed only goes so far. The main threat to the cheetah today (aside from speeding tickets) is human. Without action by governments and wildlife organizations, cheetahs could become extinct! It's up to you to help save these magnificent speed demons.

80 miles per hour
(129 km/h)

Bicycle

Think your paper route takes too long? Hop on a bicycle like *this*.

Actually, you don't hop on this kind of bike, you climb *into* it.

These bikes don't look like the sort you can buy in any old department store. *Everything* about them is different.

They're called *streamliners*. You ride by leaning way, way back inside a thing that looks like a squashed sausage, with just the teeniest bit of the wheels poking out of the bottom. All of this is to minimize wind resistance. Some bike designs are even *more* streamlined by eliminating the bubble through which the driver looks out altogether. You see where you're going on a video screen.

Streamliners are breaking all kinds of records for human-powered vehicles — hitting speeds from 60 miles per hour (97 km/h) to more than 80 miles per hour (129 km/h), these fly-by-day athletes and their rides set new records today just so they'll have something to break a week or two later.

Not only speed but distance records are being broken by streamliners. In 2006, on a flat racetrack in California, Greg Kolodziejzyk (just call him Greg K), set a human-powered distance record of 647 miles (1,041 km) in one day! That would make a *really* long paper route.

Which brings us to the question of the engine. No teardrop-shaped, high-tech marvel is worth a thing unless the human inside it is in top physical condition. So what are you doing reading this book? Get out there and deliver some papers!

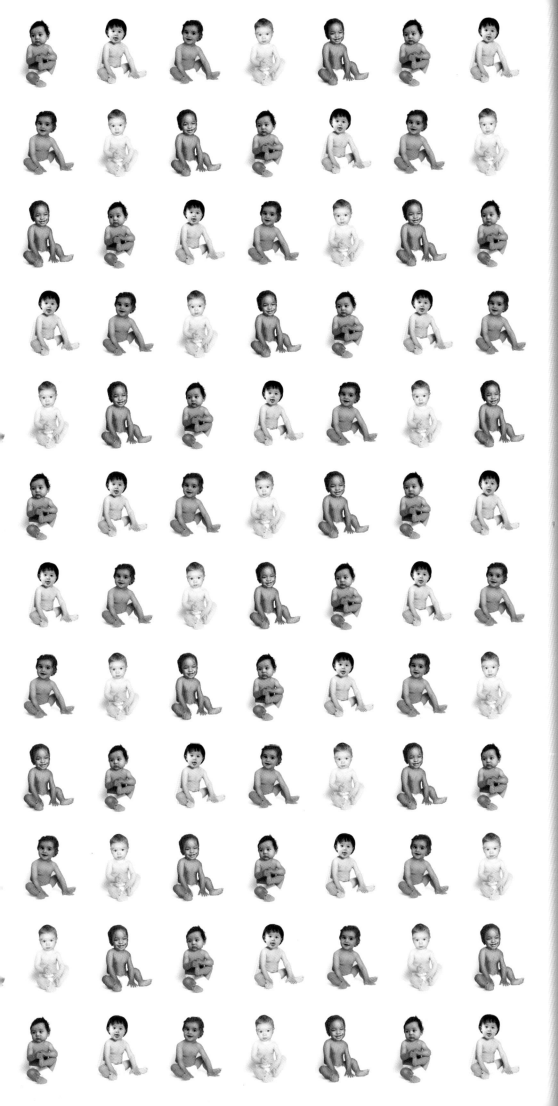

Population

Babies are cute. At least, most people think so, and that's a good thing, because there are around 250 new babies born every *minute*. In the time it took you to read this far, nearly 50 new babies have been born! That's a whole lot of newness! A hundred hands, a hundred feet!

With all these babies being born, the world's population keeps growing faster and faster. Right now, there are more than 6 billion people in the world. Where did they all come from?

Good question! Ten thousand years ago, at the dawn of civilization, there were about 5 million people in the whole entire world. That's the same number of people who now live in the metro area of Atlanta, Georgia.

One thousand years ago, in the Middle Ages, there were about 300 million people in the world. Then the population started increasing, very slowly, for about 500 years, so about the time Columbus was landing in the Americas, there were about 500 million people. Three hundred years later, around the time that Washington was President of the United States, the world's population had doubled to 1 billion!

In 1945, by the end of World War II, there were 2.5 billion people — which means that in 150 years, the world's population more than doubled again! Sixty years after that, in the year 2005, there were more than 6 billion people! If the world's population keeps growing so fast, finding places to put all the new babies may be quite a challenge.

Not to mention the diapers.

25

40 miles per hour
(64 km/h)

Coyote vs. Roadrunner

You may be surprised to learn that some television cartoons show events that have nothing at all to do with reality! But before you throw down this book and start writing an indignant letter to the television networks, let's see how bad it really is.

Take the case of the old roadrunner cartoon, which some of you may have seen.

The roadrunner is quite a zippy bird. Sprinting across the ground, it has a top speed of around 17 miles per hour (27 km/h). Occasionally, a roadrunner does fly, but only for a few seconds, and only when it's going downhill or when it's being chased by a predator (a wily coyote, for instance).

But flying is not one of the things that roadrunners do best, and they seldom take the trouble. Running is their thing. And they are fast — fast enough to catch a rattlesnake! Very fast! But not fast enough.

The coyote is a member of the dog family — and dogs, as you know, love to run. A coyote can run at speeds up to 40 miles per hour (64 km/h). It's hard to stop a hungry coyote. Desert coyotes love to hunt small mammals, reptiles, and yes, roadrunners.

To catch a roadrunner, a real coyote never has to use exotic techniques like dropping a safe off a cliff, blowing up the road with high explosives, etc. None of this is necessary because a real coyote runs more than 20 miles per hour (32 km/h) faster than a roadrunner! Let's face it: The coyote gets the roadrunner every time.

And by the way, real roadrunners don't say *beep-beep*, either.

13 miles per hour
(21 km/h)

35 miles per hour
(56 km/h)

Birds Gotta Swim, Fish Gotta Fly

Some animals don't do as they're told. Birds are supposed to fly. Fish are supposed to swim. Now meet the penguin and the flying fish. They've turned the rules topsy-turvy.

You've probably seen films of penguins doing their clumsy waddle on the ice. This activity is what scientists call *terrestrial locomotion* (walking). For penguins, it's not easy. A typical waddle keeps them going at around 1 mile per hour (1.6 km/h).

But did you ever see a flock of penguins underwater? They look just like a flock of birds flying through the air — swooping and diving with extraordinary grace in a beautiful undersea ballet — all the while gorging themselves on delicious krill.

Emperor penguins can swim in short bursts at 13 miles per hour (21 km/h) — more than twice as fast as an Olympic swimmer!

But flying? Penguins don't do that at all. They leave that job to the fabulous flying fish.

Like most fish, flying fish do not like to be eaten. But when a predator approaches, they have a wholly different way to escape.

First they swim as fast as they can near the surface of the water. Then they shoot through the surface and quickly start beating the water with their tail at more than fifty times per second! This launches them into the air where they turn into gliders by extending their huge pectoral fins — zipping through the air at more than 35 miles per hour (56 km/h), sometimes for as much as 650 feet (200 m)! And most certainly avoiding ending up as lunch.

Sometimes it pays to break the rules.

29

1,040 miles per hour
(1,674 km/h)

Earth

Fasten your seat belts! You're living on a planet that's racing through space at astonishing speed!

If you're sitting at the equator — maybe in some science class trying to stay awake — you might think you're going nowhere. But you're not! You're actually zooming at 1,040 miles per hour (1,674 km/h). That's how fast the surface of the earth is moving at the equator as the planet rotates on its axis. So why don't you have to hang on for dear life?

Because Einstein's theory of relativity says the only thing you feel is *acceleration*— the thing that pushes you back in the seat when your car starts moving faster. But the earth rotates smoothly at a constant speed so you don't feel a thing. The only acceleration you feel is *gravity*. You're constantly falling toward the center of the earth! Feel it? Good thing the ground is there to keep you in place.

By the way, in addition to falling toward the center of a rotating planet, you're also racing around the sun at an average of 66,616 miles per hour (107,208 km/h)! Fast? You're *also* whirling around the Milky Way galaxy at 486,000 miles per hour (782,000 km/h)!

Since the Big Bang, the universe has been constantly expanding. How fast does that make you go? This question can't be answered simply because *everything* is moving away from *everything else*. The farther something is located from you, the faster it's moving away from you — *no matter where in the universe you are*. The Big Bang isn't an explosion *in* space. Space *itself* is expanding. Strange? It's all relative.

Milky Way

486,000 miles per hour (782,000 km/h)

Sun

66,616 miles per hour (107,208 km/h)

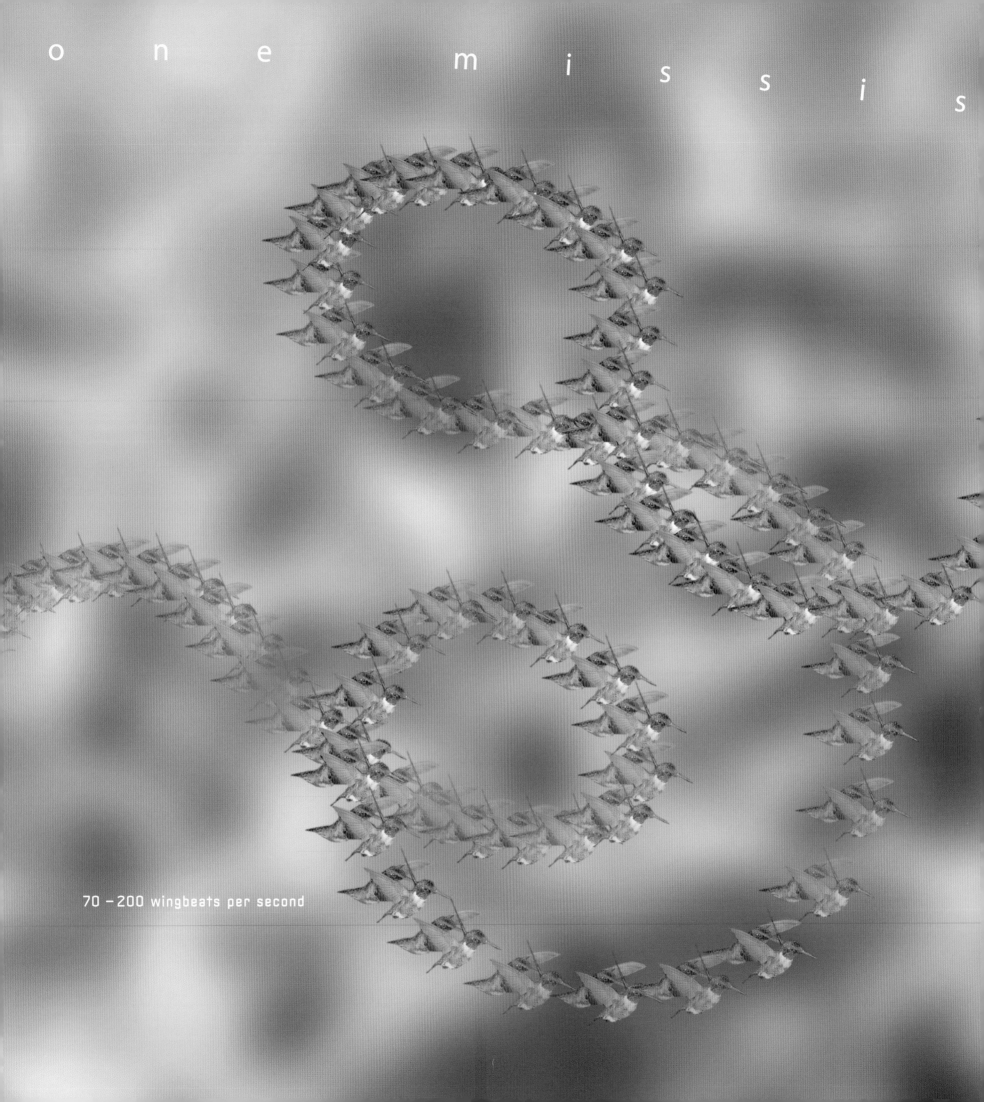

one missis

70 –200 wingbeats per second

s i p p i

Hummingbird

How many jumping jacks can you do by the time you say "one Mississippi"? That's about one second long — almost time enough for you to raise your arms from your side to over your head.

But wait! *Hmmmmmmmmmmmmmmm!*

What *is* that sound? That's the hum of power — the humming result of the blur of hummingbird wings beating. As it hovers near a flower or feeder, you might see a hummingbird very clearly, except for the space on either side. What is that haze of movement? It's hummingbird wings beating faster than your eye can see! A ruby-throated hummingbird beats its wings between 70 and 200 times per second!

Don't think that sounds fast? Get a stopwatch and flap your arms. How many full flaps can you do in a second? Half? One? Hummingbirds may be small, but everything about them is superfueled and lightning fast!

What powers those wings in flight? Tiny little hummingbird hearts thumping and pumping along at more than 1,200 beats per minute in tiny little hummingbird chests!

Why do hummers hum? Hummingbirds are the only species of bird that can really hover in midair — that's how they get at delicious flower nectar. They can even fly backward!

Hovering can take a lot out of a bird. You try it and see how far you get! To keep moving, hummingbirds have to eat a lot. In fact, most eat as much as their entire weight in a *single day* — something not to try at home.

60+ miles per hour
(1,220+ km/h)

Whip

Crack! Why does a whip make such a loud sound? You might think it's just the whip snapping against itself. That's a good guess. But the answer is way more amazing than that. The whip goes *crack* for the same reason that a supersonic jet goes *boom!* — they're both breaking the sound barrier!

How is that possible? How can you make a sonic boom with a flick of the wrist?

Well, you don't need a cowboy hat, and you don't need a horse, but you do need a whip; and with that and a little practice, you, too, can be a sonic boom generator!

Sonic booms happen when something (a jet, for example) goes faster than the speed of sound — around 760 miles per hour (1,220 km/hr). At normal flying speeds, the jet pushes away the air in front of it — just like a boat pushing through the water makes waves. But instead of water waves, the jet creates *air* waves. And what are air waves? Sound!

When a jet breaks the speed of sound, it's going faster than the waves it's making — so fast that the waves can't get out of the way! They pile up into one giant shock wave, and when it reaches your ears — *boom*!

But can you really snap a whip so it goes faster than sound? You can!

When you first snap the whip, your arm moves fast, but nowhere near the speed of sound. However, the energy you give to the whip creates a wave — a *leather* wave. The wave shape you've made in the whip moves faster and faster as it races toward the tip — then *crack!* You broke the sound barrier!

And you didn't even have to learn to fly.

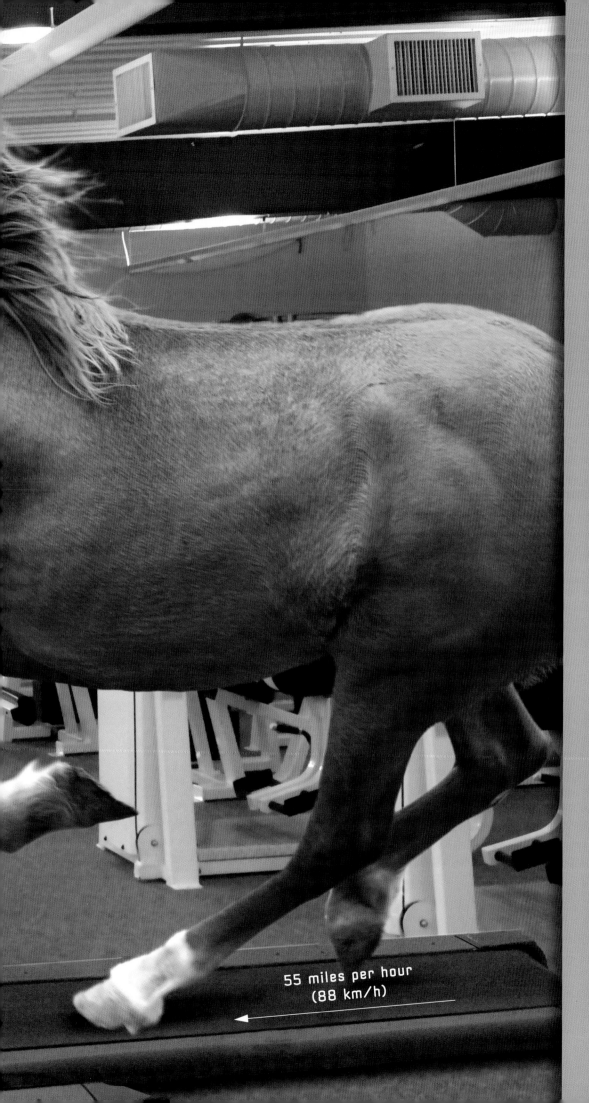

55 miles per hour
(88 km/h)

Horse

Quick, who's faster? Human or horse? The answer isn't as simple as you think.

The horse is one of the animal kingdom's most magnificent runners. On short sprints, horses have been clocked at 55 miles per hour (88 km/h). On 1.5-mile (2.4 km) tracks, they have sustained average speeds of more than 37 miles per hour (60 km/h). And in long-distance endurance races of 100 miles (161 km), horses have kept up a pace of more than 14 miles per hour (23 km/h).

How can humans even hope to compare with that? We do. Surprisingly, humans are supremely adapted for long-distance running. Most animals can leave us in the dust in a short sprint. But when it comes to endurance, a fit *Homo sapiens* can keep up with almost anything on four legs.

We are built very differently from our fellow primates, chimpanzees and gorillas, and some scientists think that it may have a lot to do with not just walking but with running.

Big hip, knee, and ankle joints, long Achilles tendons, and muscular glutei maximi all contribute to our running excellence. In addition, we have very little body hair and abundant sweat glands that allow us to cool down easily. Most animals, when they run a long time, overheat and die. Our ability to cool off allowed us to outrun our prey. We still can. In the present day, bushmen of Botswana have been seen running down kudu antelope. And in 2004, a man in Wales beat more than forty horses and riders on a 22-mile (35.4 km) course.

Humans? Slow? *Neigh!*

200+ miles per hour
(320+ km/h)

Peregrine Falcon

This bird is the fastest thing alive.

Swifter than an arrow, the peregrine falcon in its power dives goes faster than any animal on Earth — more than 200 miles per hour (320+ km/h)!

The dive of the peregrine is called a *stoop*. Here's how it works: The falcon starts its hunt as high as possible, perching on some towering object such as a cliff. When it picks out its prey, it launches into the air and tries to get above its target. This often results in a spectacular aerial contest with both birds spiraling up in a corkscrew path, each attempting to get higher than the other.

If the falcon gets the advantage, it rolls over into a dive like a fighter jet, pulls in its wings to minimize air resistance, and plummets toward its prey like a feathered missile, pulling up at the last moment to strike — either by raking its razor-sharp back talons across its victim, or balling its talons into fists and knocking the bird out of the sky.

No airplane in existence can match the aerobatic feats of the peregrine falcon. Every part of this bird is fine-tuned to allow it to perform stunning airborne maneuvers. The wings and tail can rapidly bend, curve, fan out, and change shape to allow the falcon to make lightning-fast turns and twists.

And it's built extra tough. When a peregrine pulls out of its stupendous dive, it withstands twenty-five times the force of gravity (25 g) — three times the amount that can cause blackouts in trained fighter pilots.

If ever a bird was a flying ace, this is the one.

100+ miles per hour
(160+ km/h)

Sneeze

This is it. Game point in the final game of the biggest tennis match in history. The server bounces the ball once, twice, then lofts it in the air and . . .

Ka-pow! A huge explosion! His opponent is down, flat on his back, knocked to the ground! What was that?! A lightning bolt? A meteor?

No, he sneezed!

That's right, a sneeze can fly through the air at more than 100 miles per hour (160 km/h)! The sneeze is not only as fast as a tennis ball, it's far more deadly. A single sneeze can launch as many as 40,000 infectious droplets, capable of spreading viruses and bacteria such as the Spanish flu — which killed as many as 50 million people from 1918 to 1919.

No one says "Bless you!" after a violent tennis serve — but for more than a thousand years, we have blessed one another after sneezing. Why? No one knows exactly how this started. One guess is that some people believed that sneezing caused a momentary pause in the heartbeat and left a person's soul vulnerable. With the growing understanding of the role sneezes play in the spread of disease, the custom took on new meaning: "Get well!" (Of course, some people think "Bless you" really means "Stop sneezing on me and spreading germs all over the place!")

You might wonder if you can really use a sneeze to gain an advantage over your tennis opponent. You could, but please don't. It's not polite. And just to be safe, cover your mouth when you sneeze. Please.

1 mile per hour
(1.6 km/h)

NASA Crawler

Goo.

Baby learn crawl. Baby crawl fast. Baby reach speed of more than 1 mile per hour (1.6 km/hr)! Faster than the speed of the mighty NASA Crawler-Transporter — one of the slowest vehicles ever made.

NASA has a fleet of two of these super-slow vehicles. Their only job is to move the Space Shuttle on its Mobile Launcher Platform from the Vehicle Assembly Building to the launchpad.

Did they ever have a drag race between their two Crawlers? I doubt it. It would be too dull to watch. The Crawler takes five hours to go on its 5-mile (8 km) journey — moving more or less at the speed of your baby sister.

But while the Crawler is carrying a launch platform the size of a baseball diamond — and a space shuttle — with a combined weight of almost 20 million pounds (9 million kg), your baby sister is only carrying you-know-what in her diaper. So she's got a bit of an unfair advantage.

If you're looking for something to drive that gets great mileage, forget the Crawler. It gets about 42 *feet* (13 m) per gallon when cruising down its little highway (called the *Crawlerway*, naturally). Who knows what mileage it would get in stop-and-start traffic?

Since the two Crawlers were built in 1977, they've rumbled a combined total of 2,526 miles (4,065 km). That's around the distance between Cape Canaveral, Florida, and Los Angeles, California. Ready for a cross-country trip that would take more than 100 days? Then climb aboard.

39,000 miles per hour
(63,000 km/h)

NEXT REST AREA
17 TRILLION MILES

Voyager

Uh-oh.

"Didn't I tell you to go to the bathroom *before* going into interstellar space? But do you listen? No. It's like talking to a wall! Tough luck, kid. We're going as fast as we can, but you'll just have to wait."

You're looking at the Voyager 1 — one of the fastest spacecraft ever made.

It was launched on September 5, 1977, from Cape Canaveral, Florida, aboard a Titan-Centaur rocket. Its twin, Voyager 2, was launched sixteen days earlier.

Voyager 1 has since passed Voyager 2, and has now gone farther from Earth than anything ever made by humans. In fact it's already three times more distant than Pluto — more than 10 billion miles (16 billion km).

The Voyagers are unmanned vehicles that were sent on a mission to visit the outer planets. If you *did* take a family vacation on Voyager 1, which you *can't* because there's no *air*, you would have visited the giant planets Jupiter and Saturn — and used Saturn's gravity to fling yourselves toward the edge of the solar system and on toward the stars. Right now you'd be tootling along at 39,000 miles per hour (63,000 km/h)!

Voyager 1 is now so far from home that it takes more than nine hours for a radio signal traveling at the speed of light to reach Earth. But since the Voyager itself is traveling away from Earth at only 0.00006 the speed of light, it will take a little more time to reach the next star in its path. You'll get there in around 40,000 years.

Can you hold it that long?

186,282.397 miles per second
(299,792.458 km/sec)

Light

Don't be late for school!

If you were late getting to your bus stop, making the bus run way behind schedule, you might ask your bus driver to go at the speed of light. That's the fastest speed there is.

If you politely make this request, without jumping up and down and hollering, this is what your bus driver would tell you:

"The speed limit of the universe is exactly 186,282.397 miles per second (299,792.458 km/sec).

"But the truth is, the bus cannot go at the speed of light. Only things with no mass (such as light) can go that fast. Ordinary matter can never reach light speed. Even your fastest school bus. Disappointed? Don't be.

"The bus could go very *nearly* at the speed of light. And then very strange things would start to happen.

"First of all, the bus gets squished. Do you get flattened between the seats like a sandwich? No, because *space itself* is getting squished. To you, everything looks normal, but to someone watching from outside, you're thinner than a tortilla.

"Second, everything gets heavier. To someone looking in the window, your mass is approaching infinity! You'd break every scale in the galaxy!

"Third, time slows down. Why? Because Einstein said so, that's why! So sit down and be quiet or you'll be stuck in seventh grade for the rest of your lives!

"And if you make me explain relativity theory one more time, I'm stopping this bus!"

Index

Credits

2 Boy: Richard Sands
5 Ostrich: BIOS Denis-Huot M. & C/Peter Arnold Inc.;
Bicycles: Tony Lewis/Striner/Gettyimages
7 Train: Jon Arnold Images/SuperStock;
Desert: Georgeburba/Dreamstime.com;
Cowboys: Nicholas Rjabow/iStockphoto.com,
WorldWideImages/iStockphoto.com,
Jim Parkin/iStockphoto.com
9 Brain: Richard Sands; Brain legs: amygdalaimagery/
iStockphoto.com; Computer: Digital Vision Ltd./
Superstock; Computer legs: millsrymer/iStockphoto.com;
Track: Ben Hillman
11 Baseball Field: Richard Sands;
Sloth: Wolfgang Feischl/iStockphoto.com
13 Thrust SSC: Andrew Washnik/Corpricom, Ramsey,
NJ; Plane: Stephen Strathdee/iStockphoto;
Road: Alexander Hafemann/iStockphoto
15 Window: Richard Sands; Window box: Ben Hillman;
Bamboo sprout: Siamimages/Dreamstime.com;
Buildings: Ben Hillman; Bamboo: Ben Hillman
17 Florida: NASA
19 Traffic: Richard Sands, Ben Hillman;
Fish: Aqua Paparazzi Inc., LA, CA
21 Cheetah: Eric Isselée/iStockphoto; Cop: Brand X/
Superstock; Car: Joseppi/Dreamstime.com;
Sign: Ben Hillman
23 Street: Robert Elias/Shutterstock;
Bicycle: Greg Kolodziejzyk/www.adventuresofgreg.com;
Newspapers: Ben Hillman
25 Babies: Arekmalang/Dreamstime.com,
Umbar Shakir/iStockphoto.com, Katharine Adams,
Karens4/Dreamstime.com, Brandon Clark/
iStockphoto.com; Stopwatch: Ben Hillman
27 Desert: Sally Wetzler; Coyote: Robert Deal/
iStockphoto.com; Roadrunner: Jill Fromer/
iStockphoto.com; Skate: William Fagan/iStockphoto.com;
Rocket: Xavi Arnau/iStockphoto.com;
Bomb: Perry Kroll/iStockphoto.com; Anvil: Ben Hillman;
Dynamite: Stuart Pitkin/iStockphoto.com;
Safe: Jgroup/dreamstime.com
29 Penguin: Bill Curtsinger/Nat Geo/Gettyimages;
Flying Fish: Doc White/Nature Picture Library;
Clouds: Ben Hillman
31 Driver: Richard Sands; Earth: NASA;
Milky Way: NASA/JPL-Caltech/R. Hurt
33 Hummingbird: Russell C. Hanses/Peter Arnold Inc.;
Flower: Elizabeth Buttler, Ben Hillman
35 Cowboy: Darrell Gulin/Corbis;
Jet: Nickr/Dreamstime.com
37 Horse: Mary Morgan/iStockphoto.com;
Gym: Richard Sands
39 Falcon: Mike Lane/Alamy; Archer: Richard Sands;
Background: Ben Hillman
41 Tennis Player: Julian Finney/Staff/Gettyimages;
Ball: Ben Hillman
43 Crawler: NASA; Baby: Eugeny Shevchenko/
iStockphoto.com
45 People: Richard Sands; Voyager: NASA/JPL;
Kepler supernova: NASA; Sign: Eric Bechtold/
iStockphoto.com; Bike: Ronald Bloom/iStockphoto.com
47 Bus: Ben Hillman; Background: Ben Hillman

Special Thanks: James Adams; Katharine Adams;
Antoine Alston/Berkshire South Community Center;
Andrea Angrum/JPL; Simon Ban; Gabe Bartalos;
Elizabeth Buttler; Julie Anne Collier/Wingmasters;
Michael Connelly; Jeff Dilks; Ethan Ellenberg;
Tony Gualtieri; Dan Green/Harvard Center for
Astrophysics; Tom Gasek; Melissa Hart & Judd Bortner;
Dr. David Hillman; Dr. Manny Hillman; Ruth B. Hillman;
Honey; Dwayne Howard; Dr. Jerry Kooyman/
Scripps Institution of Oceanography; Ryan Larkin;
Yasmin Northrup; Katherine Oberwager; Garnet Ord;
Pittsfield Dukes: Mitchell Duggins, Nelson Gomez,
Jeff Lieneck, Justin Leveillee, Mike Marron,
Chester Wilson; Maria Pizzuro-Cleary; Jennifer Rees;
Richard Sands; Matthew Sermini; Jim Spieler;
Robert Taylor.